SING OUT LOUD

BOOK III

Owning Your Voice

Jaime Vendera &
Anne Loader McGee

VP

Vendera
Publishing

Vendera Publishing

Interior Design by Daniel Middleton | www.scribefreelance.com
Cover Design by Molly Burnside | www.crosssidedesigns.com
Photo detail: Abby Hunter, Emi Jo Hammond,
Kirk Gilbert and Tommie Armstrong
Copyright © 2011 by Kevin Hoops | Impressive Studios
Pencil Drawings by Valerie Bastien
Audio examples recorded by Jaime Vendera

ISBN: 978-1-936307-10-4

"HEY LADY"
Used by permission
Words and music by
Scott Jason with Clayton Stroope
Copyright © 2002
Thriving Ivory Music Publishing, ASCAP

Books by Jaime Vendera

Raise Your Voice Second Edition
The Ultimate Breathing Workout
The Ultimate Vocal Workout Diary
Voice RX
Vocal RESET
Extreme Scream series
Online Teaching Secret Revealed
Unleash Your Creative Mindset

Books by Anne McGee

Strengthening Your Singing Voice (Elizabeth Sabine)
The Mystery at Marlatt Manor
Anni's Attic

Contents

Introduction

Welcome to *Sing Out Loud Book III: Owning Your Voice*. After plowing through two books focused on vocal technique we hope you're as excited as we are to start singing. First, we must applaud you for patiently working through the *Sing Out Loud* techniques for at least two months, while waiting to get into this next part. Now it's time to reward you for all your patience and hard work. Let's start singing!

Special Note: This book comes with a series of audio files, which were created to guide you through the vocal examples in this book. (**All bold words in parenthesis**) refer to an accompanying audio track, which you'll find at: http://venderapublishing.com/sing-out-loud-book-III/

Chapter 1
Setting Your Singing Pace

The first order of business is to open up and brush off your old recordings of your song from *Sing Out Loud Books I* and *II*. As you continue to apply the *Sing Out Loud* techniques you'll use that song as your 'guinea pig' song throughout *Book III*. We promised you that learning all the technical information and practicing all those crazy sounds and exercises would serve a higher purpose. Well, that higher purpose has arrived and it's time to put what you've learned to use.

We know you've sung your song over and over again, but now we'll apply style as well as technical expertise. By combining style and vocal technique, you'll soon discover you can mold your voice into an instrument that really fits you. Some of you may be tired of your "practice song". If this is the case, feel free to add a second song, but be sure to keep working with the original practice song as well.

If you choose a second song, pick one that suits your voice in your current vocal range to prevent strain. If you've been practicing the *Sing Out Loud* exercises and singing, you should have noticed your range has increased and some songs that used to be difficult are now easier to sing. I know we've said this many times, but it bears repeating: *one of the most important things to remember about singing is to always pick songs that suit your voice.* After you've completed *Sing Out Loud Book III*, you may try other more challenging songs.

You must be willing to commit to singing your practice song(s) every day now as you study this book. When applying the *Sing Out Loud* vocal techniques, don't forget to maintain your vocal energy throughout the entire song. By that we mean, sing it with all your heart and don't fade out toward the end of a line or phrase. Every word you sing is just as important as the next one.

How do you know if you're fading out or losing vocal energy? Gauge yourself by listening to the original artist as you sing along to the song. If you can still hear the singer holding the note after you've stopped singing, it's a sure sign you've faded out too soon. Sing the entire phrase and don't end the vocal line until the artist does. If you've been practicing your breathing techniques and exercises, this shouldn't be a problem. Make sure your vocal energy is just as strong on the last word of a phrase as it is on the first. Keep that vocal energy up by drinking in a cupful of air, adding breath support and feeling the buzz.

Now the real work begins. Although we want this to be a fun adventure, we also want you to become better each time you sing your song, so it's important you record yourself singing your song once every day as you work through this book. Listen back to each recording and take notes on all your vocal strengths and weaknesses. Your daily goal is to build up your strengths while correcting your weaknesses. By recording daily, you'll have proof you're improving. Save and label each file by date, and store the files in your folder.

Assignment #1–Recording Time Again

Put this book down and re-record your practice song. Compare the new version to the versions from *Sing Out Loud Books I* and *II*. Remember, it doesn't matter whether you record yourself in a studio, on your cell phone, or with a webcam. Just get your song recorded so you can begin comparing future recordings against the recording from the day before. If you follow your critique notes, you'll begin noticing substantial changes in your voice as you progress. If you've chosen to add a second song, record that as well before moving on. We'll wait for you while you do this . . . Great, we see you've recorded your song. Now, let's move onto the next chapter.

Chapter 2
Singing With Passion and Emotion

N ow you've re-recorded your song, it's time for experimentation. You are officially your very own "mad scientist" project and it's time to create your vocal "monster". First, play the original track of the song (not your version of it), and listen to the singer in a way you've never listened before. This means LISTEN. Do NOT sing along with the artist; just listen quietly. We know you've already done this fifty times in a row in *Sing Out Loud Book II,* but now it's time to step up your game. With that said, it's assignment time.

Assignment #2–Knowing Your Song Inside and Out

Write out the lyrics to your song, even if you already know them by heart. Writing will implant the lyrics so deeply in your memory that you'll remember them, even in your sleep. After you've written out the words, replay the song five times in a row as you read along, line by line. This step is extremely important because "seeing" the words as you're "hearing" them assures you'll understand the *meaning* of the song. Every song is telling a story, and you'd be surprised how many people can sing a song over and over again and yet not have a clue as to what the song is really all about. If you don't know what your song is saying, you'll never sing it with feeling and emotion. After you've read the lyrics and listened to the song five times in a row, start another document to be added to your *Sing Out Loud* folder and answer the following questions.

1. What story is the song telling?
2. What do you like about the song?
3. What don't you like about the song?
4. What emotion is the singer expressing in the song? (Is the singer excited? Does he/she sound angry, depressed, or happy?)
5. What emotion does the song stir in you? (Does it make you want to cry, jump for joy, or scream out loud?)

6. What parts of the lyric do you like the best?
7. Do you dislike any of the lyrics? Why?
8. Why do you like this song?

To sing a song to the best of your ability you must truly understand what that song is actually about. Just singing the lyrics and mimicking another singer's style isn't enough to win over an audience. You must believe what you're singing and the only way you can sound believable is to sing the song as though it's a story from your own personal life; one told with passion and in your own voice. And this passion is best summed up into three basic singing emotions:

1. **Pain**
2. **Anger**
3. **Excitement**

The quality of the voice is greatly enhanced by emotion. Good singers support every song with passion. They make singing a total emotional experience. You know when you hear an emotional singer whether they are happy, angry, or sad. The emotion portrayed in a song affects how you feel about that song. For example, one love song will make you want to cry, which is a form of pain, while another love song will get your heart racing with the excitement of love. On the other hand, certain up-tempo songs can make you feel like jumping up and shouting and throwing a party. This is because you can hear and feel the passion in the singer's voice. There are tricks to help create more passion when you sing. For instance, simply holding out a note for a long time can stir in the listener a deep sense of feeling.

Before moving on though, review which emotion your practice song best expresses, or which emotion you feel when you listen to it. You must master the emotional aspect of a song, because without that, you'll never be able to tell a compelling story or convince your listeners what you're feeling. Mastering the emotional voice will separate a mediocre singer from a great singer. Now, let's cover each emotion so you can convince your fans what you're trying to convey.

Pain

Emotional pain comes in several different forms from slight sadness to total depression. Think about a time when your friend moved away or someone broke up with you. You felt a lump in your throat and a knot in your stomach as you held back the tears, right? Now take that same feeling and project it into your sad song. Just don't let it affect you to the point of ending up with a lump in your throat. A singer's job is to maintain a positive emotional attitude while being able to quickly portray a different emotion in another song. But for now, all we want you to do is express that "sad" emotion, not take it on. It's like acting; you're pretending to be upset, when in reality you aren't. Pain comes in many forms–from having your feelings hurt, stubbing your toe, being betrayed by a friend, or being away from a loved one. (**Pain Example**)

Anger

Anger can be expressed through aggressive vocals, such as screaming, grit, wailing or shouting. When trying to create the passion of anger in your song, you must first create the feeling of hurt and then build it into anger. Think of a time when someone hurt you, or when you were really mad about something. You felt it deep down in your gut, right? Now think of a different memory. How about a time when you stubbed your toe on a rock or got stung by a bee? Remember how you cried out in frustration and the pitch of your voice went really high? Maybe it even got so loud you could shatter glass (like Mr. Jaime Vendera can do). That emotion was released as passion and energy, and all in the same breath. It's the same kind of uninhibited intense energy that a baby lets out when it cries and wails in its crib. (**Anger Example**)

Excitement

Excitement is the happy emotion where you express love, enthusiasm, and eagerness. Remember the times when you started laughing and couldn't stop? Remember how it felt and sounded? It was probably like the thrill you felt the first time you rode a roller coaster, or went down the slide at a water park. As you laughed and screamed and had a great time, your voice became buoyant and the sound floated out of you effortlessly. Just so you know; it takes less muscle to smile than it does to frown, so use your smile to add some happiness to your voice when you sing. Smiling will also give the visual effect of being happy and excited.

Take for example the picture of Emi singing below on the left. As she's singing into the microphone, she has a slight smile. It not only releases any vocal tension, but it also lets her open up her mouth so she can clearly enunciate the words.

Now for all of you rockers who are afraid that smiling will ruin your bad-boy reputation, you can alter the smile to look like you're ready to shout at the world, like Tommie is doing in the picture on the right. He looks like he's screaming his brains out as opposed to smiling, and it still helps to release vocal tension.

Excitement comes in many forms. It can be expressed in the sound of happiness in your voice to intense shouting about your feeling for a new love. Many upbeat love songs will pull at your heartstrings and make you feel excited to be with your boyfriend or girlfriend. (**Excitement Example**)

Assignment #3–Listening for Emotion

Now that you've got a grasp on the basic emotions, it's time to put this book down and read your lyrics once again as you listen to your practice song. This time, you want to really focus on the emotion in the singer's voice. What emotion is he/she trying to express? Now, recall a specific time in your past when you experienced that same emotion. Sing the song once again while holding onto that personal memory. If you can feel that emotion when singing, an audience will hear it in your voice and you'll be on your way to becoming a better singer. If you don't believe us, sing the song to someone who has heard you sing it before. Ask them what sounds different about your voice this time.

Assignment #4–Recording Emotion

Now it's time to record your practice song once again while adding passion. You have to do this every single day anyways, so this should be an easy assignment. Once you've finished recording your song(s), compare your "passionate" version to yesterday's recording. Did you notice any difference in your voice? We hope so. Are you excited? Good, now you're mastering emotional expression and are fast on your way to becoming a better singer. ALWAYS search for the emotion in every song you sing. Now, let's see how far we can go with this new tool as we move ahead to a new chapter.

Chapter 3
Vocal Dynamics

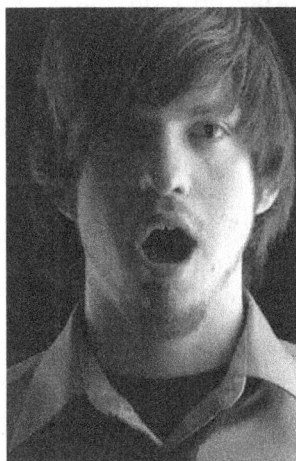

Singing a song isn't just about expressing emotion. It involves other aspects such as tone coloring and *dynamics* to make it stand out. Dynamics simply refers to how loud or how soft you sing the words in a song. It's about amplification. Take the dynamic of singing loud for example. When you sing properly, the overtones you produce will make your voice sound louder without adding excess breath pressure. Excess breath will only cause you to shout, which will hurt your voice. You must learn the difference between singing loud and shouting. (**Singing Loud versus Shouting**)

Don't be deluded into thinking that singing in a loud voice means you're singing with power. The most dangerous thing a singer can do is shout, yell, or "belt it out"–this is NOT power! The term "belting" is often misunderstood. Belting is a term that simply means to sing from the "belt" or lower waist area. This is referring to tightening the lower abdominal area to sing with volume and strength, but most singers automatically think that they must "yell" when they hear the term, "belt". You can belt without yelling, and we've already taught you how to do this in *Sing Out Loud Books I* and *II*. If you've practiced the sounds and exercises, you should have developed enough vocal power by now to shake the windows in any auditorium–and all without hurting your voice.

As mentioned earlier, if you lack power you'll only end up shouting by squeezing the throat and over-tightening the stomach muscles. For some reason, people associate clenching the throat as a way to control the voice or add more power. Trying to sing by pushing and tensing in the throat only leads to long-term vocal damage. The function of the throat is to spin vibration, not to hold the sound back in the throat.

The secret to mastering dynamics is the buzz. The bigger you can make that buzz, the easier it will be to sing louder. You do that by bringing the energy up from the abdominal area and sending it sailing out over the vocal cords. You should keep in mind that contracting the abdominal muscles to bring up more energy should never feel "forced". If it's forced, then it's wrong. Some people think that a loud singer is a passionate singer. Let's not confuse dynamics with passion, because your volume is only one aspect of adding passion. Passion means intensity in energy by combining emotion with dynamics, and not letting go of that energy.

As you begin to discover the incredible speaker system you have in your body (as you should have in *Books I* and *II*), you'll want to make sure you let all that volume out. Don't allow it to get trapped in the throat or mouth. Always feel the sound in the palate and make it a habit to drop the jaw a little when singing high notes, or when singing louder. Remember to pretend you're chewing on a huge jawbreaker at all times to keep the mouth open wide.

Now let's discuss the opposite end of the dynamic spectrum: singing at a low volume. When you sing softly, you have to sing with the same exact energy you use to sing loudly. Yes, you turn it down somewhat in volume, but that shouldn't change the focus. It actually takes more energy to sing softly than to sing loudly because of the amount of control needed to sing perfectly in tune with less breath pressure. Don't believe us? Well, then it's time for another assignment.

Assignment #5–Soft Singing

Record yourself singing your practice song again. Only this time, sing your song at your lowest volume without sounding like you're whispering. There shouldn't be any airy sound as you sing and you're not allowed to flip into falsetto. Sing in your full voice, but with the tiniest bit of volume possible. Pretend you're a fly singing the song and someone would have to listen really closely if they wanted to hear your voice. (Soft Singing)

After you've recorded yourself, you may hear little cracks or weak spots. You'll notice while singing in this low volume that it's much tougher to stay consistent, especially with regards to pitch. That's because you need to really focus on your technique and energy. You won't notice as much buzz in the palate or body when singing extremely soft, so you have to pay attention or you'll lose your focal point. Now put this book down, record your song, and then listen back to the spots where it sounds like you're vocally weak. Add more energy to those spots with more downward pressure. In other words, give it more gas. Even though you won't feel much buzz, you still want to visualize that buzzing sensation in the palate and throughout your body.

A good trick to remember is that the wider your mouth, the softer the voice. Combining a wider mouth while holding back the breath release and volume and almost speaking the words, will give you the vocal control you desire. Think of smiling while singing, or making the "eee" sound helps with that wide mouth.

Mastering dynamics is extremely important, especially when singing in the upper range. In fact, the higher you sing, the more energy you'll need and the more focus you'll have to give to keep the volume under control. You never want to have to get louder just to reach the higher notes, because that's a sign of shouting. Yes, we understand this might sound impossible because singers feel they must get louder to sing higher, but this isn't true. In time, with the aid of vocal exercise and technique, and lots of hours of singing under your belt, it will become easier to sing with less volume on the higher end.

If you still feel you need work on mastering dynamics, go back and review Assignment #9 from *Sing Out Loud Book I*. Also, spend more time doing exercise #4, the Crescendo/Decrescendo exercise. Add it into your vocal workout routine from *Sing Out Loud Book II*, right after the Sabine Power exercises. Now that we've covered passion and dynamics, it's time to move into understanding more on singing high and singing low.

Chapter 4
Singing High and Singing Low

Why do most singers make singing high or singing low so difficult? Because they *believe* it's difficult. Singing is a mental thought process and if a singer thinks a note is too high or too low, then for them, it will be. With that belief, they'll strain and reach up or look down every time they go for those notes. We do understand that each individual has a comfortable vocal range, but most people haven't even begun to discover their full usable range simply because of the fear of even trying it.

Starting right this instant, you must change your vocal attitude. Mentally repeat, "all my notes are easy for me to sing". Never imagine your high notes as going up, or your low notes as going down. Instead, see them going straight out in front of you and then coming back in again. Lots of singers think high notes go "up". You'll catch them looking up towards the ceiling when they sing high, or reaching up with their shoulders and standing on their toes. (See examples on the right.) These are bad habits you never want to develop. Most notes aren't as high as you think and by moving your vocal cords a fraction of an inch you can easily make the pitch.

When singing high or low notes, it helps to think of keys on a piano. They are laid out horizontally, which means the pianist can reach effortlessly to the left for the low notes, or to the right for the high notes. If it helps when you practice, pretend you're standing in the center of a piano keyboard. Then simply lean slightly to the left for the lows or to the right for the highs, and you'll be able to reach all notes.

Because most singers tend to think "up" when going for high notes, maybe an even better way to remember what to do is to *think* down for high notes, and up for low notes. Looks like it's assignment time again . . .

Assignment #6–Revisiting the Mirror

The TRUE secret to prevent incorrectly reaching for a high note is to practice singing in a mirror and looking directly into your own eyes. Surely, you still use a mirror when practicing, don't you? So turn on your mp3 player, fire up your practice song and sing your heart out as you watch your every move in the mirror. As you sing, do not break contact with your own eyes. By maintaining the stare as you sing, you will avoid looking up for highs notes and down for low notes. If you feel up to it, try another song, one that's a bit more challenging to push the limits of your current range. Just make sure not to strain.

Practicing in a mirror will also help break any bad facial tension habits, such as raising your eyebrows, curling your lips, not opening your mouth wide enough, etc. These are all signs of excess tension and poor technique. You should maintain a blank stare and a dropped jaw as you sing. Observe your technique. Make sure you're breathing and supporting correctly. Think of your mirror as your personal vocal coach.

Practicing in a mirror also helps eliminate neck tension. If you see the veins in your neck bulging out as you sing, it's another sign of tension and vocal strain. If you notice this, stop for a moment, take a deep breath, and re-establish your downward support. A tight neck is usually the sign of a lack of breath support, which results in the neck muscles trying to over-compensate.

A quick way to break that neck tension is by turning your head side to side as if you're saying the word "no". The "no" movement will help eliminate neck tension otherwise you won't be able to sustain the tone without your voice breaking. Use the "no" on those tough passages until you can sing them with no noticeable cracks or breaks in the voice. Assignment time again.

Assignment #7–Expanding Your Repertoire

Along with your daily exercises, you must begin singing at least thirty minutes per day while watching yourself sing in the mirror. Add four to five songs, including your *Sing Out Loud* practice song to your daily routine. Make sure to throw in a few challenging songs that reach the ends of your low and high range so you can practice the "no" trick. You can do vocal scales all day long, but unless you sing songs with low and high notes in them, you'll never learn how to sing beyond your current range. We also suggest you pick songs with different tonal colors, different emotions, and with a wide range of dynamics.

A great singer will push to expand range, color, dynamics and emotion. Are you a great singer? Prove it by singing more songs. Now let's take a book break and gather your songs before moving on. Once you're ready to move ahead, let's jump to the next chapter where we'll begin diving into the complexities of words and lyrics.

Chapter 5
Covering Consonants

Consonants are tricky little critters, yet without them we wouldn't have speech. Singers can easily lose vocal energy when they sing certain consonants because some letters stop the production of sound. This means most consonants are considered percussive sounds due to the fact that they stop airflow and do not produce tone; they are more similar to a drummer tapping the snare drum with a drumstick as opposed to a trumpet player holding out a note. But it's this use of the percussive sound of certain consonants that breaks up the drawn out tone of vowels. This is what makes a song more exciting.

The problem is these consonants are not produced at the vocal cords. They are produced with the teeth, lips, tongue and the jaw, and when you sing them, the flow of sound of the voice is disrupted because the airflow is abruptly stopped. It forces the singer to have to restart the sound of their voice with another stream of air if they want to keep on singing. Our goal in *Sing Out Loud* is to hang onto the pure sound as much as possible so the airflow doesn't have to be restarted.

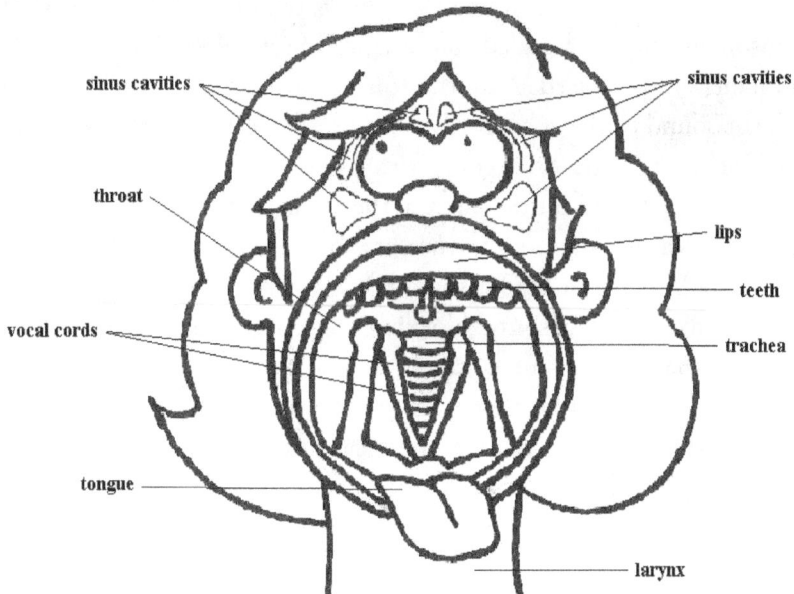

We don't want you to think the consonants are not important just because they stop the airflow. They are EXTREMELY important because they help bring out the emotional coloring needed to give meaning to words. Without them we wouldn't have such a beautiful communicative language.

Although we need to hold onto the vowels **A, E, I, O, U** when we sing, the best way to travel from note to note is by riding on a consonant. Certain consonants, such as **K, P, S** and **T** don't require any vocal cord vibration. We refer to these type consonants as "sound-blocking" consonants. Yet other consonants such as **M, N, G, Z** and **D** carry forth sound created by the vocal cords, so they're referred to as "sound-producing" consonants.

You're probably wondering what we're talking about. Simply put, sound-blocking consonants like **T** are produced while the vocal cords are not vibrating. In other words, they block your sound vibration flow. The sound-blocking **T** consonant, for instance, is created when the tongue flicks off the top front teeth or roof of the mouth and is made audible only by a small burst of air. That small release of breath can only occur when there's no sound, thus a **T** interrupts or "blocks" the vocal cord vibration.

A sound-producing consonant such as **D**, sounds similar to a **T**, but creates a barely audible pitch. In other words, the **D** consonant is basically a **T** consonant, but with added sound from the vocal cord vibration. Both consonants are produced using the tongue in the same position, but one needs the sound of the vocal cords to be heard, while the other uses breath alone. For an experiment, try going back and forth between saying **T** and **D**. If you say **D**, you can hear the pitch of the vocal cords as the **D** consonant is formed and leaves your mouth, whereas, no sound is produced by the vocal cords on the **T**. (**T and D Consonants**)

The problem with sound-blocking consonants such as **T** is that the flow of air that vibrates the vocal cords is abruptly stopped. As previously mentioned, it has to instantly restart to carry the sound. It's much easier to sing if we can sustain the sound of the vocal cords from letter to letter, word to word, and phrase to phrase. Luckily, we've come up with a solution to fix this problem.

You can replace any sound-blocking consonant with a sound-producing consonant to prevent stopping the flow of vocal energy. Let's refer back to the consonant **T** for example. When singing a **T** (like in the word "tornado"), the sound is completely stopped because **T** doesn't produce any buzz or sound. But if you replace this consonant by imagining you're singing the sound-producing consonant **D**, the vocal energy can be sustained. Now try singing the word "tornado" by thinking of it as "dornado" Do you hear the difference? It still sounds as if you're singing the word "tornado" but now it has vocal energy buzz to it, which carries the tone. (**Tornado/Dornado**)

Remember, the goal is not so much *singing* the replacement, but more of *thinking* the replacement. The following chart contains a sample list of troublemakers and the replacement consonants you can use to make them sound better.

C	=	sing it with a *g*	Care	=	Gare
			Crazy	=	Grazy
F	=	sing it with a *v*	Feel	=	Veel
			Flip	=	Vlib
H	=	keep it silent	Hair	=	Air
K	=	sing it with a *g*	Kart	=	Gard
P	=	sing it with a *b*	People	=	Beoble
Q	=	sing it as *gw*	Queen	=	Gween
S	=	sing it with a *z*	Sunrise	=	Zunrize
			Shave	=	Zhave
T	=	sing it with a *d*	Times	=	Dimes
			Trace	=	Drase
X	=	say it like *eggs*	Extra	=	Eggsdra

You'll notice we even changed the entire spelling of each word to get rid of the sound-blocking consonant. Consonants can put magic in our words, but try to get on and off them as quickly as possible, even after you learn how to substitute the sound-producing consonants. In other words, don't try to sustain your consonants. Always get as quickly as you can back onto the vowels. Holding consonants, even the sound-producing ones, won't help you create the buzz. In fact, it will dissipate any buzz you might have created.

Assignment #8–Switching Consonants

For an experiment, rewrite the lyrics to your practice song, replacing all sound-blocking consonants with sound-producing consonants using the chart above. After you've finished re-writing the song lyrics, re-record it using your new lyric sheet as a guideline. As you sing the song, keep in mind that no consonant should ever be louder than the vowel preceding it. Although you're using the new sound-producing consonants, the vowels are the key to carrying the song. Speaking of vowels, let's move on to the next chapter.

Chapter 6
The Trick to Singing Vocals

If you thought consonants were tough, vowels are even tougher. Vowels are what create your sound and if not perfected, can greatly inhibit vocal quality. As you know, singing words is nothing more than speaking words, but with long drawn-out vowels. In the English alphabet the vowels are **A, E, I, O, U**. All the other letters are considered consonants. Vowels give the voice its quality and expand the buzz; they hold all the emotion of your songs. Unlike singing consonants, however, you want to stay on vowels as long as you can.

Let's discuss the different vowels, how they are produced, and what they can do for your sound. Keep in mind that to attain the flow of vocal energy, you must sustain the vowels. That's what keeps the vocal cords vibrating and the palate buzzing.

Short Vowels

A	-Should sound like the "a" in "Fat"
E	-Should sound like the "e" in "Pet"
AH	-Should sound like the "a" in "Father"
EH	-Should sound like the "e" in "Feather"
I	-Should sound like the "i" in "Pit"
O	-Should sound like the "o" in "Top"
U	-Should sound like the "u" in "Pup"

Long Vowels

A	-Should sound like the "a" in "Play"
E	-Should sound like the "e" in "Sweet"
I	-Should sound like the "i" in "Pie"
O	-Should sound like the "o" in "Toe"
U	-Should sound like the "u" in "Juice"

(Vowel Examples)

The ultimate goal when singing lyrics is to sustain from vowel to vowel like a pencil that doesn't lift off the page. Another way to think of it is to imagine singing your song like a train moving on a track. The wheels never leave the rails.

Still, there are situations where vowels can cause problems, much like consonants. When singing words that begin with a vowel, such as "apple", "ironic", or "everything", make sure it doesn't sound like your vocal cords are slapping together. This is called *glottal shock* and considered a form of vocal abuse. When singing a word that begins with a vowel, simply add a small "y" consonant in front of it. For example, "yapple", "yironic", and "yeverything" would prevent glottal shock. The "y" consonant should barely be noticeable, if at all. This will allow you to go smoothly into the vowel without blocking the airflow from glottal shock. **(Glottal Shock and Small Y Examples)**

An alternative to adding a 'y' to words that begin with a vowel is to hold the last consonant of the preceding word and carry it into the next word. For example, if you're singing the words, "When a love like this . . ." hold on to the "n" consonant of the word "when" and run it into the next word, in this case the "a". It will sound something like this: "Whenna love like this . . ." It will make the word "a" sound like "na", but it will carry you through without a break in your lyrics and without losing any vocal buzz. Bottom line is, it's the vowels that produce the buzz, so hang on to your vowels and buzz, buzz, buzz! **(Last Consonant into Vowel Example)**

There are also words that contain combination vowels known as diphthongs. These can be one or two vowels that come together so quickly they're considered to be one syllable. **"I"** is the most famous example of this. Although **"I"** is considered one of our main vowels, in reality it's a diphthong, comprised of **"ah + ēē"**. This causes the singer to change the shape of the mouth so they can sing both vowels of a diphthong on a sustained note. Here is a list of the basic diphthongs, which should be sung in the following ratio:

Single Vowel Diphthongs

      A as in "Play" = eh + ēē (10:1)
      I as in "Kite" = ah + ēē (10:1)
      U as in "Cute" = ee + ōō (1:10)

Double Vowel Diphthongs

      OI and OY as in "Join" = oh + ee
      OU and OW as in "Mouse" = ah + oo
      OW as in "Low" = oh + oo

So, let's explain what we mean by "ratio". In the first example, **A = eh + ēē = 10:1**, you hold the first vowel of the diphthong, in this case the "eh", ten times longer than the second part–the "ēē". (**Diphthong Examples**)

These are just basic guidelines in order to give you a better understanding of how certain vowels should be sung. You don't have to spend hours memorizing these vowel sounds or struggling over the ratio. Just keep in mind the basics of what we've discussed.

Assignment #9–Discovering Vowels

Today before recording your practice song, write out your lyrics and highlight each vowel. Say each word out loud so you can pronounce the vowel properly. Make a mental note of the correct sound before you record your practice song, and don't forget to add the sound-producing consonants. Once you've finished the recording, listen back and then compare it to yesterday's version to see if you can notice any difference in your vowel pronunciation. Once you've finished, pat yourself on the back for a job well done, put this book away, and take a break for the rest of the day. We'll see you tomorrow in Chapter Seven.

Chapter 7
Putting it All Together

Welcome back. Did you have a great night's rest? Good, because we have something exciting and fun for you today. We're going to teach you how to apply what you've learned about vowels, consonants and dynamics through a process called 'Song Mapping'. This is a method for writing out the lyrics to a song and *mapping* the direction the song should follow. This method creates a unique visual map of each word showing you how loud or how soft to sing the word, how the word should be pronounced, when to add emotion, etc. In Song Mapping you can use everything you've learned about passion, dynamics, consonants, vowels, and vibrato by creating notes on your song sheet to break everything down into sections.

This is the best way to learn how to sing a song correctly. Song Mapping is your guide to singing the correct notes, breathing in the right places, adding vibrato where appropriate, etc. Enough talk. It's time for your homework. We're going to Song Map an entire song together. Follow along and it will all make sense. The song we'll use is called, "Hey Lady" by the band *Thriving Ivory*. We chose this song not only because it's a great song, but because the singer, Clayton Stroope has mastered the *Sing Out Loud* techniques. So, let's get to work.

Song Mapping is broken down into three main divisions:

Step I..................Writing the lyrics
Step II................Adding pitches above each word
Step III..............Adding map symbols

Step I–Writing the Lyrics

For "Hey Lady", we'll focus on the first verse and chorus, so copy the lyrics to the song shown below. It's best if you type the words, as opposed to hand writing them, and after you print it out, double space each line so you have plenty of room to add your notes. As part of the homework, you must study how Clayton sings each word of his song. Go to thrivingivory.com to listen to the song. Better yet, head to a music store or download it from iTunes.

HEY LADY

She checks her pulse, gotta know if her heart's still beating

And the hospital's not far if anything should happen here

She's bored in a week, big dreams but nothing material

And I refuse to believe that love is for the weak

I'm not vulnerable
Hey lady, don't give up on me

Don't burn your heart out love

Till we're ash over seas

Hey, lady, said I don't wanna fight

Like pretty girls need cowboys

I need you here tonight

Step II–Adding Pitches above Each Word
Some singers have a tendency to "wing it as they sing it"; they think they know the song well enough, therefore don't take the time to truly learn to sing it correctly. Singers sometimes think they know the correct pitch for each word, where to take a breath, and where to add vocal effects like vibrato. That isn't always true. Speaking of which, it's assignment time.

Assignment #10–Sing Clayton's Song
We slipped this assignment in here because before performing Step II, it's best to know what you sound like singing this song. So listen to "Hey Lady" ten times, and then record yourself singing along to the first verse and chorus of the song.

After you've recorded your version, grab a keyboard and begin figuring out the pitches for each word. If you don't have a keyboard, you can go to virtualpiano.net and use their free online piano. If you own an iPhone or other type of smart phone, there are tons of apps available (including free ones) created specifically for singers. If you don't read music, you might want to ask someone who does to help you figure out the notes. We have notated the correct notes below, but please don't cheat; attempt to figure them out for yourself first.

Now the fun part . . . To get each pitch correct, you'll need to listen to the song over and over again, pausing and rewinding as often as you need to figure out each note. You'll discover that as Clayton sings, many of the words have more than one pitch. Write each note directly above the appropriate portion of each word.

Step III–Adding The Symbols

Symbols can help a singer know when to sing in falsetto or full voice, when to increase or decrease volume, when to add vibrato, and when to take a breath. Here is a list of symbols that can be used for Song Mapping. Not all have been used in this song, and this list isn't complete because Song Mapping is a growing and evolving language; one where you can create your own symbols to help you remember parts of a song. Feel free to create new symbols that work for you as you learn the art of Song Mapping. Once you've created your own song map of "Hey Lady" using our symbol list, check your work against the song on the next page.

▲	Sing loud
<	Get louder
▼	Sing Soft
>	Get softer
↗	Slide Up in Pitch
↘	Slide Down in Pitch
~~	Vibrato
~	Small Vibrato
'	Take a Breath
Capital letters	Full voice
Lower case letters	Falsetto

Hey Lady

F#   F#   F   F   D#-D# D#   D# D# D#↗g# F
She checks her pulse~~~ 'got-ta know~~ if her heart's still

D#-C#
beating~~'

F#   F# F#- F-F   D#   D#   D# G#-G#-F   F
And the hos-pit-al's ~~~' not far~~ if   an-y-thing should

D#-C#   C#
hap-pen here ~'

F#   F#   F F F↗G#   D#   D#   D#
She's bored ~~~ in a week~~~ ' big dreams~ but

G#- F   F- D#-C#-C#
noth-ing   ma-ter- i-al~'

F# F# F#-F# F F-F   F   F D# D# C# D#
And I re-fuse to be-lieve~~ that love is for the weak~'

F F G#   F↘D#   D# C# C#
I said I'm   not   vulne-ra-ble~~'

CHORUS
G# G#-F↘   C# G# G# G#↘F F
Hey la-dy~~ ' don't give up   on   me~~ '

C# G# G# A#↘F   F↘D# C#   C# C#   D#
Don't burn your heart   out   love~~' Till we're ash

31

F-C# C#
o-ver seas~~ '

G# G#-F↘ C# G# G#-F F
Hey la-dy~~' I don't wan-na fight~'

C# F#-F# F# G# F - D#↘C# D# D# D# F
Like prêt-ty girls~~ need cow - boys~~' I need you here

C# C#
to-night~~'

The symbols in this map show when Clayton takes a breath, as well as other cool things like when he sings in falsetto, adds vibrato, slides from note to note, etc. Remember, there are symbols on our list we didn't use in "Hey Lady". We included them to give you a few symbol ideas you might add to other songs you map. When you make your map, use the blank spaces on the sides of your paper to make personal notes, like "Sing with sad voice" or "Add more excitement". Your side notes should be small sentences or one-word bullet points to remind you of the emotion needed for the song.

There are many colors to this song, but we've just given you the basics. We could have added symbols for when Clayton sang with a bit of a rasp, or made a reference to the smoky, slightly gritty voice he's known for, but rasp and grit isn't the subject of this book. If you want to learn more about adding rasp and creating grit, please read *Raise Your Voice Second Edition* by Jaime Vendera.

WANT TO EARN SOME EXTRA BONUS POINTS?

For extra credit you can take Song Mapping to the next level and change the spelling of words, as we showed you in the chapter on consonants. Here is an example of how we could change the first line of "Hey Lady":

JAIME VENDERA & ANNE LOADER MCGEE

"She checks her pulse,
Gotta know if her heart's still beating"

"Zhe jhegs er pulz,
Godda know iv er art's zdill beading"

You'll notice we left in the **H** after the words "She" and "Checks". That's because you want a little bit of the **H** sound to carry the consonant, but if the word begins with **H**, leave it silent. We don't really want you to sing this song the way we've written it, but you need to mentally think the sound-producing replacements because that will allow you to easily hang onto the sustained tone, and the song will flow much smoother.

For an additional five-point bonus, you can also highlight and rewrite the diphthongs. Take for example the first two words of the chorus. "Hey Lady" should actually be rewritten and sung as "ay-ee Lay-ee-dee". For even more credit, Song Map the entire song and add it to your daily practice repertoire. What will all these extra bonus points get you? An outstanding voice, that's what!

A NOTE ON CLAYTON:
Clayton is a very raspy and breathy singer. That's his vocal style, what you'd call, his unique voice. Please do not try to imitate his sound. We already have a Clayton Stroope, so focus on being you. Plus, Clayton has mastered the *Sing Out Loud* system and can easily sing with rasp and breath. It will take some time before you can add these vocal qualities, but as we said earlier, if you'd like to learn the art of rasp, please read *Raise Your Voice Second Edition*.

Note: You can study the complete Song Mapping system in *Raise Your Voice Second Edition*, which can be purchased from venderapublishing.com.

Assignment #11—Re-Record Hey Lady

Now it's time to user your Song Map and sing "the first verse and chorus of "Hey lady" once again. Compare this new version to your first recording. Bet you improved!

Assignment #12—More Song Mapping

Before moving on, take a week off from reading *Sing Out Loud Book III* and spend some time song mapping your *Sing Out Loud* practice song(s). Once you've created a thorough map, use it every day as your guide when recording. We can't emphasize enough the importance of daily practice and recording to develop your voice.

Now that you have a map for each song, you should be working twice as hard on perfecting your vocal technique. Since you've studied three books worth of vocal technique, understood the importance of passion, created a song map, used a mirror while practicing and singing, and created an audio thumbprint of your voice each day, there's no reason you shouldn't have vastly improved. The technique to singing well is as much about control of the *body* as it is about control of the *voice*. So while you're practicing your song, remember the following points to produce the best results:

- Always take a breath in the same spot, add vibrato where needed, go to falsetto when called for, and stay consistent.

- Follow your map and be sure to emphasize key words in the phrase or line of the song when it calls for it. Keep the vocal energy up right to the ends of the words. You never want to drop your energy and end a phrase with collapsed lungs.

- Even with your map in hand, continue to practice singing in a mirror so you can catch any facial tension. Notice if you're looking up for the high notes and down for low ones, and check that you're breathing correctly. If you notice bad habits, correct them immediately.

- Don't sing with your chin up—it clamps down on the vocal cords and strangles the sound. If you're using the mirror correctly, it's easy to prevent this from happening. Look directly into your eyes while maintaining the blank stare. If you never lose contact with your eyes, you won't reach up or down for notes.

- Remember to breathe in that cupful of air on a very quick yawn, filling the belly up and expanding out your belly, back, and ribs.

- Sing with a slight smile. It will make your voice sound warmer. Lots of rock stars sing with a smile, even the punk rockers, but they hide what they're doing with the microphone so you think they're angry. Ha, ha.

- When you sing, pretend you have no neck. This will force you to remember to sing from your abdomen and not extend your neck upwards for the high note. It will also help get your vocal energy up into the roof of your mouth (palate).

- Keep your abdominal muscles firm with downward pressure so you can support your energy. Keep your ribs out so you don't expand the chest or lift the shoulders. This prevents chest breathing and neck tension. Never let go of the downward support at any time while singing. In other words, don't take your foot off the gas pedal.

- The firmness of the legs is also very important in holding up the muscles of the mid-section as they give you strength and physical support when singing on stage. Have you ever noticed how your legs shake when you're nervous? When your knees are buckled together, you won't be able to support your voice so keep your legs spaced apart and planted firmly on the floor.

- Make sure the neck and jaw are relaxed at all times. Some singers lock their jaw and neck muscles, which is evident by bulging veins and strained facial expressions. A tight jaw will prevent the sound from being released. Keep the mouth open wide enough that you don't mumble your words. To help with this, imagine you have a huge jawbreaker in your mouth keeping your teeth and mouth open wide.

- Feel for the buzz at all times, both in the palate and throughout the body.

Phew, that's enough info, don't you think? We know your brain is packed with hearing the same technical instructions, but we did it on purpose because reading and hearing these instructions over and over again is what helps build and maintain your voice. We hope it all sank in. Before you can move onto the next chapter, though, you must spend the next week working on your song, applying your map, and developing your vocal technique. Don't forget to record daily. We'll see you back here in seven days.

Chapter 8
Developing Your Own Vocal Style

Congratulations, you've made it to the final part of *Sing Out Loud Book III*. To recap, you've learned the basics of vocal technique, mastered your emotions, and done some song mapping. Now it's time to begin building your voice by finding you own style.

So what's the secret to becoming a star?

Practice! Practice! Practice!

We bet you thought you were going to get by without hearing that, hmmm? WRONG! Now that you've been singing and applying the basics for a while, it's time to take it to the next level. This is the place where we teach you how to develop your own style. Every singer needs to have style

If our calculations are correct, you've had over two months of daily vocal warm ups and workouts while singing your practice song or songs every day. Now it's time to talk about YOUR individual vocal style. If you want to be a super star you MUST find your *own* voice. The world doesn't need another Michael Jackson, Katie Perry, Taylor Swift, or Steve Perry.

As with fingerprints, the tones in your voice are unique only to you. No matter how hard someone may try to emulate your sound, they will never be able to sing or speak the frequencies in quite the same way you do. And that's a good thing because your voice is your audible thumbprint. It separates your sound from everyone else.

Some people may sound similar to other artists, but there's no way anyone can perfectly match them, even if they have a similar physical makeup. Why? Because if you put two singers that sound almost identical side by side, you'll notice they may be different heights, have different shaped noses, or smaller heads, etc. And these physical differences affect each singer's individual tone. On top of the physical characteristics, they have each had different emotional experiences. And it's these emotional experiences that play the major role in making one's voice unique.

Now it's time to create the best YOU that you can be. Apply what we've taught you throughout the *Sing Out Loud* series and you'll begin to find your own distinctive voice and style. While a book alone will never replace a vocal coach to help you create a unique, individual style, we can give you a five-step process to get you started towards discovering your own voice. So here goes.

1. **Continue to sing the songs you love.** Singing must be fun and will be when you sing songs that excite, make you happy, or touch you emotionally. Find songs you will never grow tired of, even when you sing them over and over again.

When you sing the songs you love, don't be disappointed if you don't sound anything like the singer. We don't want you to sound like another singer. Sing along to these songs, but just be *you* as you sing them. You'll eventually find a list of songs that will fit your voice.

Sometimes there'll be singers you absolutely love and wished you sounded like, but every time you attempt to sing their songs you end up making your throat sore. If you find this is only happening when singing songs by punk or hard rock bands that add a lot of grit or screaming, it isn't necessarily that the songs don't fit your voice, it's just a sign you haven't yet learned how to scream properly. Screaming is an art form so if you want to learn an aggressive style, check out other books by Jaime Vendera, or go to screaminglessons.com to learn how to master this. The bottom line is: sing, sing, sing, and keep learning more new songs.

2. **Sing songs that suit your voice.** You know from the above paragraph there'll be songs that just don't fit your voice. This doesn't mean you can't eventually sing these songs; you just may not be ready yet or might be struggling because you're trying to imitate the singer. You must sing every song in YOUR own true voice.

You might have had one of your friends say you sound like a certain singer, so if you do, feel free to have fun singing that singer's entire catalog–assuming the singer excites you and you love singing along with them. There's nothing wrong with having similar qualities to another singer. Take the bands *Nickelback* and *Theory of a Deadman*. The first record *Theory of a Deadman* released, the singer Tyler Connolly sounded very similar to Chad Kroeger of *Nickelback*. Ironically, the first *Theory of a Deadman* release was produced by Chad Kroeger. But once the second record was released, Tyler had evolved into more of his own style and although he had some similar vocal qualities to Chad, you could still tell the difference between a *Theory of a Deadman* song and a *Nickelback* song. So have fun singing along to singers you vocally resemble, just don't go overboard, or you'll hurt your throat. Steve Augeri, who fronted the band *Journey* for ten years, sounded very similar to Steve Perry, but even he admitted it was tough trying to sound like the original *Journey* front man.

Once you've gravitated to someone you can relate to vocally, learn five to ten of their songs, then apply what you've learned from those songs to other singers you sound nothing like. For instance, if you have a sound similar to *Nickelback*, try singing a Kevin Rudolf song with the same *Nickelback* tone. But never become a parrot. Just get a similar vibe going on, and above all, quit if it hurts your throat. Once you find tones that sound cool and feel good when you sing them, keep those tones as part of your vocal bag of tricks and apply them to other songs.

3. **Sing songs from artists you DON'T like.** Now that you've gotten some vocal tricks under your belt, it's time to spread your wings. We want you to pick a song from an artist you don't like. Maybe you're a fan of the band *Train* but don't like *Matchbox*

Twenty. Or maybe you're a Kelly Clarkson fan, but don't like *Pink*. Give the artists you don't like a chance. Pick a song by them, song map it, and then learn to sing it. You'll be surprised at the new vocal tricks you'll discover simply by singing along to them. Keep the tricks that work for your voice, and discard the others. Over the course of a year, you might even fill that bag of tricks so full you'll need a second bag! And, surprise, surprise, you might even discover you like many of the artists you never bothered to listen to before.

4. Sing with all the emotions. We can't impress on you enough the importance of finding your *own* sound and not copying someone else's. Sometimes as singers we get locked into singing the same kind of songs, such as only choosing to sing sad love songs. You'll never grow as an artist if you get stuck in an emotional rut.

If that sounds like your current routine, it's time to find a number of songs that are up-tempo and happy. If you're always a "happy song" singer, then begin singing songs full of sadness, or anger. Look for different types of songs and singers to study, but keep in mind that the purpose of this journey is to find your *own* unique voice and the songs that make you sound the best.

5. Learn what works for you and what doesn't. As you continue singing, you'll learn and master new vocal tricks, such as a vocal lick, a quirky vibrato, a bit of grit, etc. After you've learned a handful of tricks, you need to listen to those tricks as you try them out in your recordings and decide what sounds cool and what works best for you. Keep the cool tricks and ditch the rest. This is how you develop your own particular vocal style.

DRUM ROLL PLEASE... HERE'S A BONUS!!!

Master Your Vibrato. Vibrato is the staple of your sound quality. When you add vibrato, it makes your voice sound fuller. Natural vibrato occurs when your voice is free of tension, but sometimes the voice needs help creating a stable floating vibrato. So we've created the *Sing Out Loud Vibrato System* just for you to master. Follow along with the vibrato audio workout and you'll own anther great tool to use throughout any song. (**Sing Out Loud Vibrato System**)

Now that you've got many songs and maps under your belt, a great warm-up/workout program, mastered the secrets to singing, and have five, uh, we mean SIX great steps for finding your own vocal style, you're ready to be a star, right?

Well, not so fast cowboy (or cowgirl), the next important thing is stage presence. That's where you learn how to own the stage so your fans will love you even more. However, that's the subject of another book, *Sing Out Loud Book IV*. But before we leave, we think you deserve one more assignment.

Assignment #13–Collecting Vocal Tricks

Today we expect you to record your last practice song, and if you've added a second song, record that as well. Also record yourself singing the *Thriving Ivory* song. Listen back to all three songs and as you listen, write down notes on what you did vocally that sounded cool. Did you add a little breath to a certain part, or did you slide up in pitch and power on the chorus? Whatever you did that you really liked vocally, write it down and begin using it in other songs you sing.

Now that we've finished *Sing Out Loud Book III*, you should take your usual month off between books and focus even more on developing your unique singing style. Listen to and sing along with TONS of songs and fill up your vocal bag of tricks. We'll see you in the next book, where we'll teach you how to own the stage.

Psst-don't forget to keep doing your vocal workout from *Sing Out Loud Book II!*

About the Author
Jaime Vendera

Jaime Vendera is the author of a variety of books and one of the most sought-after vocal coaches on the planet. Using the methods he created, Jaime turned his two-octave range into six octaves with massive decibels of raw vocal power that enabled him to set a world record shattering glass with his voice. When singers need more vocal range, power and projection, or need to build up vocal stamina to perform every night, they call Jaime Vendera. Jaime states that, "none of this would have been possible without God."

Ben Thomas of Dweezil Zappa says that Jaime is the 'Mr. Miyagi' of vocal coaches, while Mat Devine of Kill Hannah considers him more of a 'Yoda.' James LaBrie of Dream Theater said, "Because of my lessons with Jaime, my voice is feeling and sounding better than it has in twenty years. I am spot-on every night. He is the Vocal Guru." Myles Kennedy of Alter Bridge said, "One time during a tour, I was so sick I could barely make it through the set. It looked as if we were going to have to cancel the next show. Jaime spent some time giving me some tips that helped me regain my voice. By the next night, I was able to perform the show. He is fantastic! *Raise Your Voice Second Edition* is THE book for singers. I recommend his books and his private instruction to ALL singers." Jaime can be contacted at www.jaimevendera.com.

About the Author
Anne Loader McGee

Anne has studied with a number of well-known Hollywood singing teachers. She has performed in musical theatre productions and taken classes in songwriting, music, and film at both the American Film Institute and the University of California and Los Angeles (UCLA).

She also co-wrote *Strengthening Your Singing Voice* with Elizabeth Sabine, a voice-strengthening expert whom many famous singers, actors, and speakers have consulted over the last twenty-five years. (www.elizabethsabine.net)

As an award winning children's writer, Anne has produced plays for young people, developed animation scripts, and had a number of short stories published in magazines, and in the Los Angeles Times. Anne's middle grade novels, *The Mystery at Marlatt Manor* and *Anni's Attic* are available at Amazon and Barnes & Noble. You can find her at www.annemcgee.com.

www.ingramcontent.com/pod-product-compliance
Lightning Source LLC
Chambersburg PA
CBHW060101050426
42448CB00011B/2564